The Zen Panda and the Moonlit Meadow

57 Stories to Calm the Mind, Find Inner Harmony,
Overcome Doubt and Realise Your Ultimate Potential in a
World of Chaos

Hiroto Takahashi

Contents

INTRODUCTION..7

The Unmoved Moon: Hiroto's Encounter with Panda 7

PART I: Calming the Mind 8

Chapter 1: The Power of Ritual in Centering the Mind 8

Chapter 2: Confronting Confusion 9

Chapter 3: Balancing Chaos 10

Chapter 4: Embracing Harmony 11

Chapter 5: Embracing Ephemerality 12

Chapter 6: Appreciating the Moment....................................13

Chapter 7: Inner Quietude..14

Chapter 8: Isolating Oneself..15

Chapter 9: Conducting Mindfulness 16

Chapter 10: Unmasking..17

PART II: Finding Inner Harmony...18

Chapter 11: Lesson from Luminous Grotto..........................18

Chapter 12: Secrets in the Sand 19

Chapter 13: Ceremony of Being...21

Chapter 14: The Pumpkin Paradox 22

Chapter 15: Of Fireflies and Mysteries................................23

Chapter 16: The Mechanical Forest......................................24

Chapter 17: The Sigh of the Ancient Mountain.....................25

Chapter 18: The Symphony of Stillness 27

Chapter 19: The Alchemy of Kindness..................................28

Chapter 20: Unbreakable..30

PART III: Overcoming Doubt..**32**

Chapter 21: Embrace Impermanence................................32

Chapter 22: Cultivate Beginner's Mind 33

Chapter 23: Practice Mindfulness..................................35

Chapter 24: Non-Attachment..36

Chapter 25: The Middle Way 37

Chapter 26: Paradoxical Thinking 39

Chapter 26: The Panda's Revelation 40

Chapter 28: Question the Ego.......................................42

Chapter 29: The Illusion of Control.................................44

Chapter 30: The Unwatered Seed....................................45

PART IV: Realise Your Ultimate Potential **46**

Chapter 31: The Forgotten Pages 46

Chapter 32: Limitless Becoming.....................................47

Chapter 33: Unveiled Potential 48

Chapter 34: Luck – Action - Reaction 50

Chapter 35: Zazen and Mindfulness 51

Chapter 36: Mindful Alchemy 52

Chapter 37: Infinite Circles of Awareness..........................54

Chapter 38: The Unseen Orchestra..................................56

Chapter 39: Training Ground...57

Chapter 40: Gym 58

PART V: In a World of Chaos..**60**

Chapter 41: Social Media Overwhelm...............................60

Chapter 42: Environmental Crisis 61

Chapter 43: Political Unrest 63

Chapter 44: Work-Related Stress... 65

Chapter 45: Consume Culture.. 66

Chapter 46: Relationship Troubles....................................... 68

Chapter 47: Personal Illness or Injury 69

Chapter 48: Family Responsibilities 71

Chapter 49: Commuting Chaos 72

Chapter 50: Public Outrage, Cancel Culture 74

PART VI: Beyond The Meadow.. 76

Chapter 51: In a Realm of Pure Energy................................. 76

Chapter 52: An Unanswerable Question 77

Chapter 53: The Ethereal Chamber 79

Chapter 54: Beyond the Horizon 81

Chapter 55: The Unknowable.. 82

Chapter 56: Nirvana... 84

PART VII: Panda's Final Koan... 85

Chapter 57: Oneness.. 85

ABOUT THE AUTHOR 86

BONUS #1 Exclusive Offer... 88

BONUS #2 Meditation & Mindfulness Material................... 89

INTRODUCTION

The Unmoved Moon:
Hiroto's Encounter with Panda

In the quiet heart of a bustling universe lies a tranquil meadow, bathed in the light of an unwavering moon, here, in the embrace of nature's soft lullabies, I found the embodiment of all I had sought: the Zen Panda. This gentle creature, with its deep eyes and unhurried grace, became my mirror, reflecting the inner serenity I had longed to achieve.

Our world is often a swirl of chaos, pulling us in every direction, making it difficult to find our centre. Yet, in the simple presence of the Zen Panda, I discovered the profound truths hidden within the ordinary, the calm amidst the storm. This book unfolds as a tapestry of stories that chronicle my journey with the Zen Panda, as we explored the mysteries of the mind, faced the shadows of doubt, and danced to the silent rhythm of inner harmony.

To you, dear reader, I extend an invitation. Walk with us through the moonlit meadow, listen to the wisdom of rustling leaves, and let the tales of the Zen Panda guide your spirit to a place of peace. May you find, as I did, the still point in a turning world, and recognize the unmoved moon that resides within us all.

PART I:
Calming the Mind

Chapter 1:
The Power of Ritual in Centering the Mind

There was a tea house on the outskirts of Kyoto and the Panda arrived amidst a grove of whispering bamboo. The night was stitched with stars, and a crescent moon watched silently from above. Lured by the soft light of lanterns and the inviting scent of green tea, the Panda entered.

Inside, an old master sat on a tatami mat, engrossed in the delicate stages of a tea ceremony. With a nod, he invited the Panda to sit across from him. The Panda did, and the master resumed his ritual—boiling water, measuring tea leaves, and elegantly pouring the hot liquid into a finely crafted cup. Each movement seemed to fold effortlessly into the next, a wordless poem of grace and precision.

Panda quietly watched, its restless thoughts began to settle, captivated by the master's tranquil choreography. Once the tea was prepared, the master slid the cup toward the Panda. Taking a sip, a wave of warmth spread through its body, quenching the noise of the mind for a suspended instant.

The master and the Panda locked eyes briefly, communicating an unspoken understanding. The Panda then dipped its head in a gesture of respectful farewell.

And so, in the realm between actions and words, in the pauses that punctuated each movement and sip, something indescribable yet profoundly calming took root. The Panda rose, bowed to the master, and then simply was its presence echoing the serenity it had discovered, a sanctuary without walls.

Chapter 2: Confronting Confusion

Just outside the bustling city of Barcelona, a curious Panda found itself standing before an intricate garden labyrinth. The towering hedges seemed like a secret language, their curves and angles promising both enigma and revelation. Compelled by the mystery, the Panda took a deep breath and entered.

Panda navigating the pathways, felt neither urgency, nor confusion. Every twist and turn were a moment to be fully lived, not a puzzle to be solved. The air was thick with the scent of blooming jasmine, and the Mediterranean sun dappled the ground, casting kaleidoscopic patterns that seemed to dance in tandem with the Panda's steps.

Eventually, the Panda reached the centre of the labyrinth where a lone olive tree stood, its branches laden with silver-green leaves that shimmered in the sunlight. The ground was a mosaic of broken tiles, fragments of stories long forgotten. The Panda felt a sense of completeness, an inner stillness that seemed to resonate with the serene atmosphere of this hidden sanctuary.

Turning to leave, the Panda found that its journey back to the entrance was equally harmonious. The labyrinth, once an intricate maze, now felt like a familiar friend, its paths an extension of the Panda's own tranquil mind-set.

Before it knew it, the Panda had returned to where it started, standing at the threshold that separated the labyrinth from the outside world.

Emerging into the sunlight, the Panda stepped forward, its presence echoing the calm clarity it had discovered. There were no walls, no puzzles, just a pathway that extended in all directions, inviting the Panda to continue its journey wherever it felt led to go.

Chapter 3: Balancing Chaos

As the Panda balanced on a surfboard off the coast of California, facing the mighty waves of the Pacific Ocean, nearby surfers transformed the powerful expanse into a playground, their graceful manoeuvres upon the water forming an impromptu community, which danced with the ocean.

Initially unsteady, the Panda wobbled as the waves ebbed and flowed beneath it. However, it soon noticed how the seasoned surfers used the ocean's force to their advantage. They didn't fight the wave but rode its energy, melding their movements with the natural rhythms of the sea.

Inspired, the Panda took a deep breath as another wave rolled in. Leaning into the swell, it gripped the board tightly with its feet. Far from being overwhelmed, the Panda felt elevated, carried by the wave in a fleeting but exhilarating rush of tranquillity and thrill.

The wave dissipating into froth, cheers erupted from the surrounding surfers. The Panda was back in calmer waters but carried with it a profound sense of change. Waves would come and go, as would life's various challenges, but it was one's attitude and approach that determined the experience.

With fresh wisdom in its heart, the Panda glided smoothly back to shore. Now, instead of fighting the ocean's rhythms, it felt like a part of them—a harmonious note in the grand symphony of life.

Chapter 4: Embracing Harmony

The dimly lit ballroom in Buenos Aires held observing Panda and the tango dancers, who seemed to weave unseen pictures through their synchronized movements. The atmosphere pulsed with the intimate chords of the bandoneón, and the Panda was fully captivated, feeling as if it were the sole witness to a deeply personal conversation between the dancers.

Fascinated, the Panda felt a pull toward the dance floor. Hesitant but curious, it stepped onto the hardwood, accepting an invitation from a seasoned dancer. Initially, its steps were clumsy, but the dancer didn't pull away. Instead, they guided the Panda subtly, allowing it to match their tempo.

Once the music swelled, something transformative happened. The Panda began to understand its partner's cues not as commands but as invitations. Each step turned into a word, each glide into a sentence, and soon they were having a conversation—not with voices but with movement.

When the song reached its crescendo, the applause from the crowd seemed miles away. The Panda felt an inner sense of balance and unity that it had never felt before. As the dance concluded, it stepped back, nodded gratefully to its partner, and made its way off the dance floor, carrying a quiet but profound sense of equilibrium back into the bustling world.

Chapter 5: Embracing Ephemerality

Beneath the vast expanse of the Sahara night sky, the Panda sat entranced. The atmosphere was thick with tranquillity, punctuated only by the soft, distant howls of desert winds. A telescope was perched nearby, manned by a local astronomer inviting by-passers to glimpse into the cosmos.

Feeling a magnetic pull, the Panda approached the telescope. The viewfinder revealed dazzling planets, sparkling stars, and far-off galaxies. As it watched the celestial ballet unfold across the sky, a soothing calmness spread throughout its being. It was a silent but profound reminder of the universe's grand scale, making the Panda's earthly woes appear almost trivial.

Taking a step back, the Panda felt its mind effortlessly quiet down. It seemed to join the eternal waltz of celestial bodies, relinquishing its transient anxieties to the grand depths of the universe. A shooting star dashed across the heavens, a fleeting moment of light that vanished as quickly as it appeared—a reflection of life's ephemeral worries.

Resting on the soft desert sands, the Panda continued to observe the starry spectacle, allowing the universe's endless cycle of light and darkness to wash over it. As the Panda looked up at the celestial panorama, a peaceful clarity replaced the mental chatter, as if it too had become a small yet integral part of the universe's grand design.

Chapter 6: Appreciating the Moment

Nestled in a quaint Swiss chalet, the Panda gazed through the window at a world transforming under a soft snowfall. Each snowflake that landed on the wooden ledge was unique, a silent masterpiece of nature's design. A roaring fire crackled in the background, but even that seemed muted by the absorbing silence outside.

For the Panda, time seemed to slow. It was almost as if the universe conspired to create these perfect moments, these crystalline fragments of time that spoke more than a thousand words. The Panda decided to step outside, feeling the cold air kiss its fur as it wandered onto the porch.

Here, surrounded by towering pine trees and steep, snow-covered mountains, the Panda felt an overwhelming sense of smallness. But unlike before, this realization didn't unsettle its mind; it enhanced the stillness within. Each snowflake became a silent symphony, a momentary work of art that formed, existed, and then seamlessly melded into the larger landscape.

The Panda extended its paw to catch a snowflake, marvelling at its intricate design before it melted away. It was as if this single, fleeting moment encapsulated a timeless wisdom, whispering the art of finding tranquillity by cherishing the transient, unrepeatable moments that made up life's grand tapestry.

Returning to the warmth of the chalet, the Panda carried that silence within, forever imprinted by the simple understanding that peace wasn't something to seek in the outside world. It was there, in the stillness that bloomed when one took the time to truly be present, to appreciate the wonder tucked into each transient moment.

Chapter 7: Inner Quietude

High above the cacophony of New York City, atop a towering skyscraper, amidst a rooftop garden stands the Panda. Skyscrapers pierced the heavens around it, each a monument to human ambition. Everywhere, the city pulsed like a restless heart—neon signs flashing, vehicles honking, people in a perpetual rush.

A jazz musician on another rooftop sent a plaintive melody into the sky. For a brief moment, the Panda closed its eyes, absorbing every note. When it opened them, a falcon soared by, an embodiment of grace amid chaos. It circled once above the Panda, as if sharing a secret, before disappearing into the skyline.

It was as if the universe had orchestrated these moments just for the Panda, a private symphony of sight and sound. And yet, inside, an inexplicable quietude reigned. The Panda was neither detached from its surroundings nor swallowed by them. It was there, fully present, yet deeply calm. It had discovered an oasis of serenity that no external conditions could disturb.

As the city transitioned from the golden glow of sunset to the electric blues and purples of evening, the Panda felt no urge to move. Time stretched and contracted around it, a rubber band that held no sway over its inner world.

Finally, as the moon rose like a silver medallion over the city that never sleeps, the Panda stood up, not to escape the noise, but simply to continue its journey. In its heart, a calm as ageless as the moon itself had settled, a quietude that would remain, no matter where life took it next.

Chapter 8: Isolating Oneself

Far from familiar bamboo forests, the Panda walks a glacier of the world's southernmost tip. A landscape of frozen majesty stretched in all directions, eerily quiet except for the occasional creak of shifting ice. Towering icebergs floated in a nearby sea like sculptures in an otherworldly art exhibit.

It had come here not by plan but by some internal compass, an urge for a solitude so profound it seemed to have been sculpted by the hand of the divine. For what seemed like days, the Panda walked, leaving behind it a trail of paw prints soon to be erased by snow and wind. Yet, it didn't feel lost. For the first time, perhaps, it was getting closer to finding itself.

A sudden wind howled across the glacier, as if trying to speak to the lone wanderer. The Panda sat down, facing the wind squarely, its thick fur rippling like a flag. And then, the strangest thing happened. The wind seemed to pass right through it, as if it had become as transparent as the ice around.

It was a moment of epiphany. Alone on this icy expanse, far from any living being, the Panda felt more connected to the universe than ever. All the questions that had been swirling in its mind seemed trivial now. It was as if the glacier had absorbed them, freezing them into insignificance.

With a newfound sense of self, almost as if it had shed an invisible layer of old skin, the Panda stood up. As it looked around, everything seemed to be in sharper focus the sparkling ice, the clear sky, even the distant stars seemed to wink in acknowledgment. There was no need to go anywhere, no urge to do anything; for the first time, it was fully present in its own existence, a silent guardian of its own soul.

Chapter 9: Conducting Mindfulness

Behind the crimson curtains of Vienna's famed opera house, the Panda sat in a plush armchair. The air buzzed with anticipatory electricity, yet the backstage was a realm of orchestrated chaos: singers warming up their vocal cords, musicians tuning their instruments, stagehands bustling with props and set pieces. Despite the whirlwind of activity, the Panda sat still, ears finely tuned.

As the conductor raised the baton and the orchestra unleashed the first notes, the Panda felt the vibrations of the strings, the trumpets, and the timpani resonate through its being. It listened intently, not just to the individual instruments but to the symphony they created when woven together. Highs and lows, crescendos and decrescendos, all flowed in a seamless, intricate tapestry of sound.

It was during a quiet interlude, when a single violin played a mournful melody, that it struck the Panda. Each note, whether soft or loud, fast or slow, had its perfect place in the composition. No sound was more important than another; all were essential for the symphony to be whole.

The Panda realized that its mind operated much the same way. Thoughts and feelings were like musical notes, each with a role to play in the greater composition of its consciousness. When it tried to suppress the dissonant notes of sadness or amplify only the harmonious notes of happiness, the inner symphony lost its balance.

As the final act came to a close and the performers took their bows amidst a thunder of applause, the Panda felt not just a sense of peace but an awe for the delicate balance of life's complexities. Here, in the symphony's blend of chaos and harmony, it found a striking, sublime resemblance to the intricate compositions of its own mind.

Chapter 10: Unmasking

Amongst the vivid colours and elaborate costumes of Venice's grand carnival, the Panda got drawn to a mask-maker's stand. Hand-painted masks with feathers, jewels, and intricate designs beckoned from every corner. Visitors swarmed the stand, each selecting a mask that spoke to their hidden desires or fantastical imaginations. Even though it was an outsider amidst the spectacle, the Panda felt an urge to belong and reached for a mask of sparkling azure and gold.

Slipping the mask over its face, the Panda joined the parade of costumed revellers through narrow streets and across ancient bridges. Gondolas glided over the waterways, and joyous laughter filled the air. Yet, the Panda noticed something odd. Behind the mask, its senses felt duller; the laughter seemed more distant, the colours less vibrant.

Curious, the Panda found a quiet nook overlooking a moonlit canal and took off the mask. It observed the festival's reflections in the water: the shimmering lights, the fluttering masks, and the people hiding behind them. It then looked at its own reflection and saw clarity and tranquillity in its eyes, a stark contrast to the disguised mayhem around it.

The Panda returned to the festival but left the mask behind. As it walked through the celebration unmasked, it felt an inner freedom that was overwhelmingly liberating. The lights seemed brighter, the laughter more genuine, and the experience more authentic.

As the clock tower chimed to signal the festival's end, the Panda felt more connected to the world around it and, more importantly, to itself. It didn't need a mask to experience life's grandeur. It realized that true liberation comes not from the masks we wear but from our courage to remove them.

PART II:
Finding Inner Harmony

Chapter 11: Lesson from Luminous Grotto

In the heart of a tranquil meadow bathed in the soft glow of fireflies, Panda felt a surge of curiosity and existential wonderment. Suddenly, the earth beneath him began to hum softly, and before he knew it, he was no longer standing on solid ground. He found himself gently pulled into a whirlpool of colours and sensations, descending through layers of water, and arriving in an underwater grotto surrounded by glowing coral and luminous fish.

Here, the walls were made of living coral, ever-changing in hue, and the floor was a bed of iridescent seashells. A seahorse, its scales shimmering like precious stones, greeted him. "Welcome to the Luminous Grotto. May your questions find their current and your answers find their tide," it said, gesturing him to sit on a clamshell.

"Thank you," replied the Panda, his eyes widened by the wonder around him. "Where I come from, I'm part of a forest, part of a family. Here, I feel like a droplet lost in an ocean."

The seahorse swirled a fin, and a bubble filled with what seemed like liquid moonlight floated towards him. "Ah, the riddle of magnitude. The ocean is vast, and we feel minute. But consider this: isn't it wondrous that we, merely droplets, have the capacity to contemplate the sea?"

The Panda tasted the liquid moonlight. It was like drinking the essence of a tranquil night—calm, serene, with a touch of mystery. "True," he mused, "but the enormity still weighs heavy."

"Visualize your life as this bubble," the seahorse elaborated, "limited in the scope of the ocean, yet teeming with its own qualities—its luminescence, its buoyancy, its unique path. Every bubble matters to the sea it belongs to. Likewise, your life has significance, uniqueness, and intent."

As the Panda contemplated this, he felt a subtle shift within him. The wisdom was simple, yet deeply impactful. "Thank you," he said, feeling a renewed sense of inner balance.

As he spoke these words, the grotto gradually melded back into the fabric of the ocean, leaving him enveloped in a tranquillity that was as boundless as it was intimate. The next moment, he found himself back in his firefly-lit meadow, a realm as mundane as it was miraculous, and he knew he would never perceive it—or himself—in the same way ever again.

Chapter 12: Secrets in the Sand

The Panda found himself enveloped in a strange light, its shimmer pulling at the very fibres of his being. When the light subsided, he looked around in awe and confusion. No longer was he in the moonlit meadow or the interstellar teahouse from his previous adventures. Instead, he stood at the threshold of an endless desert, its sand dunes rolling like waves in an ocean of golden grains. The sun bore down unrelentingly, and the air was dry and still, its silence almost palpable.

He felt a sudden pang of vulnerability. There was no bamboo to munch on, no shade to rest under. The barren landscape was far removed from the lush forests and serene meadows he was accustomed to. Confused but intrigued, he pondered, "Why have I been brought to such a harsh environment? What lessons could this emptiness possibly hold for me?"

Eager to find answers, he began to wander and soon met a contemplative trio: a wise old tortoise, a seasoned camel, and a vibrant cactus. Each seemed to be in a deep, meditative state.

The Panda approached them cautiously. "I'm lost, both literally and figuratively. How do you all find harmony and wisdom in what appears to be such an inhospitable place?"

The tortoise opened his eyes slowly and replied, "Ah, do you see the desert as empty? The oasis may be dry, but the soil remembers its moisture. Stillness has its own rhythm."

The camel added, "The absence of sandstorms isn't a lack; it's a gathering of potential. This landscape teaches us patience and the transformative power of nature."

Finally, the cactus said, "The dim moon has its purpose. It gives us the opportunity to appreciate both the darkness and the light."

Absorbing their wisdom, the Panda realized the desert was not a void but a space filled with untold lessons. And just as he arrived at this understanding, the sky darkened, and rain began to replenish the dry oasis, while winds gathered in a dance of sand and the moon illuminated the night sky anew.

"Embrace the emptiness, for it is full of wisdom," the tortoise remarked.

Feeling enlightened and more attuned to the world's hidden harmonies, the Panda thanked his new friends and continued his journey, the desert's silent wisdom now etched into his soul.

Chapter 13: Ceremony of Being

In the ancient village of Shenjing, where the verdant hills met the meandering river, lived a humble tea master named Lin. His tea house was nestled beside a centuries-old willow tree, its branches lazily swaying with the wind like an enlightened monk in meditation.

Every morning, Lin brewed tea from leaves collected from the Sacred Lotus Mountain, never missing the subtle symphony each leaf performed—each note unveiling a secret about the universe. But despite his profound understanding of tea and life, Lin often found himself entangled in webs of anxiety, searching for an elusive inner peace.

One auspicious day, a wandering monk named Dao entered the tea house. After sipping Lin's meticulously brewed tea, he smiled and remarked, "Ah, the essence of the universe in a cup, yet you seem disquieted, my friend."

Lin sighed. "I seek inner peace, yet it's like trying to grasp the wind."

Dao chuckled softly, "Inner peace is not something you seek, it's something you cultivate. Your tea leaves don't worry about tomorrow, nor lament yesterday. They simply unfurl in the water, releasing their essence."

Lin's eyes widened as if seeing the world anew. From that moment, he brewed each cup not as a means to an end but as an end in itself. His days became a continuous ceremony of being—each moment, each breath, each drop of tea an affirmation of his newfound inner peace. And thus, Lin became the epitome of tranquillity, a master not just of tea, but of life itself.

Chapter 14: The Pumpkin Paradox

In a quaint meadow dotted with wildflowers, Panda found himself in the presence of an enormous, resplendent pumpkin. This pumpkin was unlike any other, as large as a small cottage and radiating a sort of glow that was neither sunlight nor moonlight. Intrigued, the Panda circled it, unable to fathom its grandeur compared to the other pumpkins he had seen before.

After a moment's contemplation, he settled down next to it, feeling dwarfed. However, the more he looked, the more he noticed the complex patterns on its surface—tiny grooves, irregular patches of colour, and minuscule insects going about their day as if the pumpkin were a world of its own. It was then that a ladybug landed on his paw, momentarily locking eyes with him before taking off back to its pumpkin universe.

The Panda´s eyes widened in realization. To him, the pumpkin was just a part of his world, remarkable but still a single entity. To the ladybug, and surely other creatures like it, the pumpkin was a universe, teeming with life and opportunities. The scales of importance were relative; what was colossal and extraordinary to one was commonplace and ordinary to another.

This simple observation sparked a thought in the Panda mind. Just like the pumpkin and its tiny inhabitants, every being, every place, and every moment held its own universe of possibilities and perspectives. Each had its own story, and each story was equally valid, no matter how insignificant it might seem to others.

Feeling a newfound respect for the myriad universes that existed within his own, the Panda stood up. As he lumbered away, he cast one last look at the pumpkin—his gigantic gourd of wisdom—and smiled.

Now, wherever he went, the Panda carried with him the lesson of the pumpkin: that perspective is relative, and that which may seem trivial to one could mean the world to another. And so, he moved through his own universe, humbled and wiser, forever cherishing the lesson he had learned from a day spent beside an extraordinary pumpkin in an ordinary meadow.

Chapter 15: Of Fireflies and Mysteries

Longing for a change of scenery, the Panda had meandered through various landscapes before finally finding himself in the heart of a tranquil bayou. It was as though he had stumbled upon an untouched world, far removed from the hurried pace of everyday life. Settling down on a soft bed of moss, he looked forward to what the evening would reveal.

The Panda felt the silence around him deepen as hundreds, perhaps thousands, of fireflies took to the air. They danced a luminous ballet, orchestrated by an unseen hand, illuminating the bayou in a spectacle of ephemeral brilliance. Each tiny light flickered for only a moment before disappearing into the night, only to reappear elsewhere, as if playing a celestial game of hide-and-seek.

As he watched the fireflies, the Panda felt a stillness wash over him, a tranquillity born of a deep, inexplicable understanding. Each flash of light, as brief as it was, bore testimony to life's transient nature—here for a moment, gone the next, and yet profoundly beautiful in its impermanence.

It struck him then, in that moonlit cradle of nature, how the fireflies mirrored life itself. Just like their transient glow, each moment of life was both ephemeral and infinitely precious, never to be repeated. It was in that fleetingness that the real beauty of existence lay—a beauty that was easy to miss in the endless pursuit of permanence.

The fireflies' lesson was not lost on the Panda. As dawn edged its way into the bayou, gradually dimming the fireflies' glow, he rose from his mossy seat, forever changed. He felt grateful, not just for the grand, enduring aspects of life, but also for its fleeting, evanescent moments.

Carrying this newfound understanding in his heart, the Panda ambled away from the tranquil bayou, ready to embrace the beauty in life's ephemerality. Each fleeting moment now held a depth and richness it never had before, as if the very impermanence of life made everything more precious, more luminous, in his eyes.

Chapter 16: The Mechanical Forest

Once upon a time, Panda found himself drawn away from his usual bamboo-dining spots by an inexplicable urge. With each step into the unknown, he felt less like he was leaving something behind and more like he was answering a silent call.

The path led him to a forest where the boundary between organic and synthetic was not just blurred but beautifully intertwined. Here, metal vines and wooden limbs spiralled around each other; gears and leaves shared branches in a dance of coexistence. Even the stream ran over both stones and gears, refusing to distinguish between the two.

And then, in a quiet glade, under a tree of copper and bark, the Panda sat. Time seemed to fold in on itself. Was he there for a moment, or a millennium? The forest offered no answers, only a serene silence that hummed with the songs of birds and the whispers of turning cogs.

When he rose, it was as if he had always been standing, as if he had never left his bamboo grove at all. He returned to his home, resuming his life among familiar bamboo shoots under a sky that looked the same but felt immeasurably vast.

The Panda ate bamboo, but it was as if he tasted it for the first time and had always known its flavour. His gaze was the same, yet it carried a depth unfathomable even to him.

What was the lesson of the mechanical forest? Was there a lesson at all, or was the forest simply a mirror reflecting what the Panda had always known but never seen? And so, he ate his bamboo, under the same sky, forever the same and forever changed.

Chapter 17: The Sigh of the Ancient Mountain

The adventurous Panda, finding himself in a new realm, began to ascend an ancient mountain known for its wise spirit. As he climbed higher, the air turned colder, and the view expanded, revealing a vista that went on forever. Then, a gentle rumble vibrated through the ground and resonated in the air—a sigh, it seemed, coming from the mountain itself.

Intrigued, the Panda paused and spoke aloud, "Mighty Mountain, did you just sigh?"

From the heart of the mountain, a voice rumbled, "Indeed, young wanderer. How perceptive of you."

"What could possibly cause an ageless mountain to sigh?" asked the Panda, sitting on a flat rock.

The mountain's voice deepened, "I've seen millennia pass, and yet, everything changes but also remains the same. I sigh for the inevitability and yet the futility of all endeavours."

The Panda chuckled. "Ah, the great paradox! But tell me, if everything is so cyclical and perhaps meaningless, why do you continue to stand tall?"

"I have no choice," said the mountain. "But also, in every cycle, a hiker finds his way, a bird learns to fly, and a stream carves a new path. They bring brief but brilliant meaning to my ancient existence."

"Ah, so you find joy in the little things, the fleeting moments?" queried the Panda.

"Yes," the mountain sighed again, but this time, it sounded more like a content exhale. "And today, you've given me another reason to stand tall."

The Panda grinned, feeling lighter despite the altitude. "And you've taught me that meaning isn't just in the grand, eternal things but also in the transient, small moments."

As he continued his ascent, the Panda couldn't help but think that the mountain was also climbing, in its own way, through cycles of existence, standing tall, yet humbled by every fleeting moment that gave it a new reason to be.

Chapter 18: The Symphony of Stillness

In the heart of a bustling metropolis, where skyscrapers kissed the clouds and streets pulsated with endless activity, our Panda found himself wedged between

the cacophony of urban life and the silence of his own soul. Far from the gentle rustle of bamboo leaves, he was now enveloped in honking horns, busy footfalls, and electronic billboards screaming advertisements.

This wasn't any random city; it was Serenopolis, a place where, ironically, serenity was the most traded commodity. Everyone was busy buying peace in bottles, attending tranquillity seminars, or tuning into "24/7 Zen FM." Yet, the quest for peace had become another rat race, another hustle. The irony was palpable, and Panda couldn't help but chuckle—a little humour to lighten the profundity.

Guided by a whimsical intuition, he arrived at an old, forgotten theatre, its sign half-broken but still readable: "Orpheum." Something about it caught his attention, and the wordless beckoning was too strong to ignore. It was here that he encountered Maestro Serenata, a rabbit with a baton, who orchestrated not music, but silence.

As Maestro Serenata lifted his baton, the theatre filled with an indescribable stillness. Each movement commanded an invisible orchestra of calm, played not on strings or woodwinds but on the very air itself. The setting was otherworldly—walls adorned with cosmic frescoes, where constellations seemed to sway to the unheard music. Ah, the visual imagery was like a poem written in stardust and light!

But wait! Just as Panda began to feel the enveloping calm, a group of city dwellers burst in, smartphones in hand, demanding to record this "concert" and post it online. Their chatter shattered the stillness, and Maestro Serenata's baton quivered.

Panda felt a momentary surge of annoyance but caught himself. With a smile, he stepped up and joined the Maestro, taking up a second, smaller baton. As they both waved their batons, the room shifted from dissonance to harmony. The intruders, feeling the peace but unable to capture it on their screens, soon found themselves putting their phones away, lost in the tranquil magic. And so, a lesson unfolded, one that was not shouted but whispered: true peace cannot be recorded or bottled; it can only be lived.

Feeling a sense of unity with everyone and everything, Panda knew he had found a peaceful corner within himself. A corner that he could access anytime, anywhere, whether amidst rustling leaves or blaring horns.

As he left the theatre, his spirit was ablaze with a new realization—peace is not just something you find; it's something you become. The streets of Serenopolis never seemed the same again; they were as noisy as ever, yet carried a subtle melody of stillness that only he could hear. It was a tune he would carry in his heart, a silent anthem to the beauty of being

Chapter 19: The Alchemy of Kindness

Amidst rolling hills and sprawling farmland, Panda ambled into a quaint little village named Auroria. This was no accidental detour; he felt pulled by an inexplicable force, a magnetic charm that transcended reason. Forget bamboo forests and tranquil rivers; here, the very air was saturated with an aura of kindness so palpable you could almost taste it. It was like inhaling the scent of freshly baked bread infused with sunbeams—comforting, uplifting, and nourishing to the soul.

Upon entering Auroria, he encountered its residents, who were not just humans, animals, and mythical creatures but also walking, talking embodiments of virtues. There was Generosity, a fox distributing fruits; Compassion, a swan attending to the sick; and Joy, a sprite laughing and dancing with children. These weren't mere acts; they were expressions of their innermost selves, as natural as breathing.

Intrigued, Panda wandered into the heart of the village, where stood a magnificent tree unlike any other. Its leaves were not green but golden, and instead of fruits, it bore little crystalline hearts that shimmered in the daylight. This was the Heart Tree, the source of all kindness in Auroria. Or so it seemed until he met the mysterious Keeper of the Tree—a hermit crab wearing a shell of pure gold.

With a slight chuckle, a humorous glint in its eyes, the Keeper said, "Ah, you think these hearts grow on the tree, but it's the other way around. The tree grows from the hearts, nourished by the kindness the villagers invest in each other."

Feeling the philosophical weight of that statement, Panda had an aha moment. Kindness was not just a commodity to be harvested but a cycle, a form of alchemy that turned ordinary actions into golden experiences. When he asked how he could contribute, the Keeper offered him a crystalline heart from the tree.

"Plant it wherever you go," advised the Keeper, "and see how it transforms not just the soil but also the souls around it."

As Panda took his leave, carrying the golden heart in his paw, he knew that he had become a part of something much larger than himself—a cosmic tapestry of kindness, woven one golden thread at a time. The hills of Auroria faded into the horizon, but its essence remained, pulsing through him like a never-ending symphony.

Therein lies the whispering wisdom of this tale: Kindness is both the seed and the fruit, the cause and the effect, and in nurturing it, we partake in an alchemy that turns even the most ordinary life into a luminous adventure.

Chapter 20: Unbreakable

Amidst the towering trees and emerald ferns, Panda found himself the unlikely subject of a woodland comedy show. A group of mischievous raccoons were revelling in public mockery, satirically mimicking his slow gait and peaceful demeanour. Onlookers—squirrels, birds, and even a deer or two—had gathered, chattering and laughing at the spectacle.

It would have been easy for the Panda to feel humiliated, to react defensively, or to slink away in shame. However, he remained unfazed, calm as a placid lake, eyes twinkling with a knowing kindness.

Slowly but deliberately, he moved toward a sun-dappled clearing and began to meditate. The act wasn't a defiant challenge to the crowd but a gentle reminder to himself. As he settled into the rhythm of his breath, he felt enveloped in a shroud of inner tranquillity. He was his own sanctuary; the jests and jeers were like pebbles against a fortress, unable to disturb the peace within.

Noticing the transformation, the crowd grew silent. The raccoons exchanged puzzled glances. There was an almost palpable shift in the atmosphere—people were bewildered by the spectacle of calm that was equally as compelling as the comedy had been. The Panda had presented them with an enigma: How could someone remain so serene in the face of mockery?

Eventually, the crowd dispersed, leaving the Panda in his sunlit sanctuary, peaceful as ever. His lesson to them and to himself—was unspoken but deeply felt: True strength lies not in the swiftness of reaction but in the grace of restraint. For the Panda, the external world could toss insults and judgments, but they would always dissolve upon contact with his inner harmony.

PART III:
Overcoming Doubt

Chapter 21: Embrace Impermanence

Panda's favourite bamboo grove dries up. Initially, Panda is distressed, questioning the very foundations of his existence. However, he soon discovers a new grove different, but just as nourishing.

Panda meets Mei, a charming panda who waltzes into his life one fine day. They spend days munching bamboo and nights gazing at stars. Mei, though, is a wanderer. One day, she leaves, and Panda is again left to contemplate change.

Panda encounters an old turtle, who, seeing his contemplative demeanour, tells him, "The only constant is change. Both joy and sorrow are fleeting."

Panda observes the changing seasons. New bamboo shoots sprout, then grow tall and eventually decay, only to be replaced once more. It clicks life, in all its impermanence, is a never-ending spiral.

Coming back to where he started, yet not quite the same, Panda understands. He sits in his new favourite bamboo grove, feeling not a sense of loss, but one of awe at the eternal dance of change.

As Panda ages and his fur greys, he welcomes each stage of his life not as a feared unknown, but as a returning friend. Each year brings him back to the same seasons, the same cycles of life and death, yet every turn on the spiral offers a fresh perspective.

Through each layer of his spiral journey, Panda learns a little more about the beauty of change. With every twist, he's not quite where he was before, nor is he entirely somewhere new. Ah, dear Panda, he's become a creature of impermanence, forever spiralling through life's inevitable transformations, and in that spiral, he's found his peace.

Chapter 22: Cultivate Beginner's Mind

Once upon a time, in a scenario as surreal as a dream, Panda found himself in ancient Greece. The surroundings were alien—a city bustling with philosophers and commoners, all under a cloud of smog.

When confronted with an entirely unfamiliar setting, do you perceive it as a land of threats or opportunities? What does this say about your outlook on life?

Panda roamed the polluted streets, marvelling at the architecture and history that filled the air, despite the smog. But not all was welcoming. He sensed enmity from a gang lurking in the city's shadows.

While the city was an environmentalist's nightmare, Panda recognized something else—the people's resilience and innovation. They had created aqueducts, theatres, and laws. Could the pollution then be a cry for a solution, waiting for an open mind to hear it?

How do you approach challenges or problems in your life? Are they obstacles, or veiled opportunities calling for creative solutions?

As he explored, Panda was surrounded by the gang he sensed earlier. Their faces bore hostility, but Panda looked deeper. He saw fragments of fear, uncertainty, and the yearning for respect.

Is it possible to find wisdom even in the eyes of those who wish you harm? What lessons can adversity itself teach us? Panda thought about his tranquil bamboo forest and realized the woods had never taught him to judge, only to observe. Each plant, each creature, had a role to play. Why should it be different for these hostile Athenians?

Can your environment shape your character? How often do you question the familiar patterns and traditions you were raised with?

After a tense standoff, Panda calmly walked away. The gang was perplexed; instead of fear or anger, they sensed an indescribable calm. For Panda had learned a lesson—the beginner's mind is not a canvas but a kaleidoscope, constantly shifting and refracting light into endless patterns.

In your life, are you more of a canvas absorbing the colours thrown at you, or a kaleidoscope, reshaping and reframing experiences into new patterns of understanding? Panda eventually returned to his forest, not just as a repository of experiences but as a seeker who had unlocked the wisdom in questions. And so he realized, to cultivate a beginner's mind is to perpetually ask, seek, and wonder.

Are you willing to keep asking, seeking, and wondering, even when you think you have all the answers? What might that mean for your life's journey?

In your own life's story, what questions are you willing to ask?

Chapter 23: Practice Mindfulness

What is it that weighs down our souls like anchors to the seabed of time? Is it our fixation on a past that is forever gone or an unknown future that's yet to come? Could it be that in seeking far and wide for answers, we often miss the truth that exists here and now?

In a quaint little forest, a microcosm of personalities, lived Panda. He was the spiritual nucleus around which friendships orbited. Each of his friends—Squirrel, Sparrow, and Badger—was a universe unto themselves, teeming with questions, struggles, and, of course, doubts.

One sunny afternoon, Panda called for a meeting at Wisdom Grove, a place where the trees seemed to whisper secrets if you listened closely. But this wasn't an ordinary gathering; it was a rendezvous with the "now."

As they sat in a comforting circle, Panda spoke, "We often let our minds wander to yesterday's regrets and tomorrow's worries. These are but ghosts that haunt our present."

Squirrel twitched her tail, a sign of agitation. Sparrow shuffled her feathers, clearly uncomfortable. Badger grunted, sceptical but attentive.

Panda continued, "Let's try an exercise. Close your eyes, feel the ground beneath you, listen to the rustle of leaves, the songs of distant birds, feel your own heartbeat."

They did as told, and for a moment, the forest around them seemed to pause, acknowledging their stillness.

Opening their eyes, Panda asked, "What did you feel?"

Squirrel found her tail had stopped twitching. Sparrow felt a newfound lightness in her wings.

Badger, always the realist, couldn't deny the sense of peace that washed over him.

"My friends," Panda said softly, "Being present allows you to recognize the roots of your doubts as they arise. You don't feed them; you don't empower them. They're like seeds that cannot sprout without your attention."

In that simple yet profound gathering, each friend found a newfound strength. They recognized that the power to overcome doubt was not in some distant time or place, but in the gift of the present moment. And so, they made a pact to meet more often, not just in body but, more importantly, in mindful spirit.

Chapter 24: Non-Attachment

Once upon an Olympic moment, in an arena that echoed with the cheers and hopes of thousands, Panda found himself engrossed in a spectacle of muscle and will. But what caught his eye wasn't the athlete soaring through the air or the sprinter breaking the tape; it was Tiger, a celebrated athlete, sitting alone, his stripes glowing dimmer than usual.

"Why the long face?" Panda asked, bringing his focus to the moment, as he joined Tiger on the bench.

"I don't know if I can win," Tiger muttered. "The world expects so much. What if I fail?"

Panda sighed softly. "Ah, the grand circus of expectations. Always juggling, aren't we? Here's a thought: have you ever considered that it's not the medal that defines you, but how you engage with the journey?"

Tiger looked puzzled. "Are you saying the outcome doesn't matter?"

"In a way, yes," Panda said. "See, life's like a river, always flowing. If you try to clutch at its waters, you'll end up with nothing but wet hands. Non-attachment isn't about not caring; it's about not letting the ebb and flow of external circumstances dictate your inner peace."

As the time for his event neared, Tiger felt a strange serenity embrace him. He participated, not with the burden of expectations, but with the freedom of non-attachment. He didn't win, but neither did he lose. For the first time, he felt victorious in his pursuit rather than the outcome.

Months later, Panda bumped into Tiger, who was now a coach inspiring young athletes. "You were right, Panda," he said. "Not attaching my worth to that medal was the best thing that happened to me. It freed me."

"And how are you now, still trying to clutch the river?"

"No," Tiger chuckled. "I've learned to swim."

And so, both walked away, unburdened by the weight of golden expectations, forever floating in the river of life, but never sinking. For they understood, in the grand scheme of things, it's not about what you hold, but what you let go.

Chapter 25: The Middle Way

A single sentence can shatter or shape a world: "You're too much of this, too little of that." Ah, the perennial dance between extremes—Panda was all too familiar with it. It started when he became the head of a martial arts academy; people now described him with either reverence or disdain, but rarely anything in between.

He walks into the dojo. Disciples bow. Some eyes squint—hero-worship. Others dart—disapproval.

Amid the choreography of flying kicks and synchronized forms, he feels the heaviness. The unforgiving cycle of never being enough for some and too much for others wraps around him like a tightening knot. The dojo, once a haven of spiritual tranquillity, is slowly becoming an arena of discontent, shadowed by an echo of relentless judgments.

That evening, he visits an old Zen garden, where the yin-yang stones lay in seamless union, neither overwhelming the other. The whispering winds seem to say, "The Middle Way, my friend, the Middle Way."

He returns. Gathers the disciples. "Changes," he announces.

"From today, we balance. I've been caught up in being your perfect leader that I forgot the wisdom of the Middle Way. Forgive me," he pauses, looking at each face, reading a symphony of emotions, "as I forgive myself."

New rules. Less rigidity, more flow. No overindulgence, but no denial either.

The balance is not just in the katas they perform or the discipline they embody. It seeps into their interactions, their judgments, and most importantly, their self-views. The dojo regains its lost tranquillity, each bow now a union of respect and understanding, devoid of extremes.

Time passes. Seasons change. The academy thrives.

And so does Panda, finally unfettered by the need to be 'too much' or 'too little.' He finds a quiet joy in being just enough, just so, just balanced. The Middle Way.

So, dear reader, where do you stand—or better yet, dance—between the extremes? Remember, a single sentence can shatter or shape a world: "You're too much of this, too little of that." Or perhaps, "You're just right, as you are." Ah, the perennial dance between extremes—may we all find our Middle Way.

Chapter 26: Paradoxical Thinking

Caught in the throes of an existential conundrum, Panda blurts out, "I can't make sense of it all, master. I'm paralyzed by my own doubts and fears." This is how we find him, already deep in the courtyard of an ancient Zen temple in Japan, surrounded by cherry blossoms and engaged in a soul-searching conversation with the venerable Zen master, Roshi Fox.

Roshi Fox meets Panda's eyes and poses a question, "Tell me, is the sound of one hand clapping a noise or a silence?"

Panda's eyes narrow. "That's paradoxical; it's both and neither."

Smiling, Roshi Fox says, "Ah, so you're beginning to grasp Zen koans. They're the conundrums designed to break the cycle of your ordinary, rational thinking."

Still puzzled, Panda inquires, "So, I should abandon logic?"

"Your rational mind is the tool that's broken; paradoxical thinking is the means to fix it," Roshi Fox advises, as they wander alongside a koi pond rippling with golden and orange fish.

"As ephemeral and eternally beautiful as these cherry blossoms are, so are you. You think your existence is insignificant, but remember: No mud, no lotus. You cannot have the flower without the soil," the master adds.

Panda gazes at the koi circling in their pond. They seem to go nowhere, yet they are content. A koan flashes through his mind: "What is the colour of the wind?" Absurd but deeply meaningful, it makes clear everything and nothing at once.

The master notices Panda's contemplation. "When you achieve a state of 'mu,' or emptiness, you move beyond all doubts. There, you'll discover your answers."

As Panda departs, a newfound lightness elevates his steps. The paradoxes hadn't merely evaporated his doubts; they'd flung open doors to perspectives previously unimaginable.

Panda found his elusive truth in the quagmire of Zen paradoxes. And Roshi Fox, watching Panda's back vanish beyond the temple gates, feels the satisfaction of knowing another soul has escaped the constraints of rationality.

And you, dear reader, are you prepared to untangle the Zen knots of paradoxical thinking? If the answer is yes, realize the path already lies beneath your feet.

Chapter 26: The Panda's Revelation

In doubt, I've wandered into countless paths, yet none seem my own," Panda thought, as his paws touched the temple's ancient wooden gates. That thought floated in and out of his mind like a leaf on a pond.

Three weeks earlier, Panda found himself in the garden, hose in hand. "Ah, Upaya—the skillful means," Lobsang had said, and sent him here. Each plant he touched seemed to whisper, each leaf seemed to teach, but what?

Fast forward to a moment when Panda was adjusting the temple's thangka, imitating Lobsang. "Your path doesn't have to look like anyone else's," Lobsang's words echoed in his mind. The colours of the painting seemed to bleed into his doubt, each hue offering a different answer.

Rewind to his first encounter with chanting. The deep vocal vibrations of the monks reverberated in his soul but didn't seem to still his thoughts. Instead, it felt like a choir of questions each demanding an answer.

Back in the present, Lobsang approached him with a warming smile, "So, have you found your Upaya?"

In a rush, all those moments—the chanting, the painting, the gardening—converged. "I have," Panda replied. "In the garden, I understood. There's no single 'right' path, only ways tailored to individual souls."

Flashback to a week ago, as Panda dug into the earth, and something clicked. The act of nurturing another form of life brought him the clarity that no chant or scripture could. It was then that the grip of doubt loosened, allowing him to breathe.

The story might not follow a linear path, but then again, neither did Panda's journey towards understanding. It was pieced together from experiences, a mosaic of moments that formed the picture of his newfound clarity. His was a path made of fragmented steps, each valuable, leading him to understand the essence of Upaya—finding one's own way.

Chapter 28: Question the Ego

In the deafening roar of clashing swords and battle cries, even the bravest warriors find themselves haunted by the whisper of ego, clawing at the edges of their consciousness. "Am I strong enough? Am I a hero or a fool?" Amidst the smoke and the mud, where life hangs by a thread, the battlefield serves as an arena not just for soldiers but for their egos, duelling in the depths of their minds. In a place where mortality is constantly questioned, the ego fights its own war, jousting between the extremes of narcissistic valour and crippling self-doubt.

Here, on this ground soaked in the consequences of human conflict, we find our protagonist: a Panda, a warrior with fur as dark as the night and as light as day, embodying the eternal dualities of life. In the midst of chaos, the Panda will confront not just foes made of flesh and bone, but the nebulous adversary that dwells within—the ego, a foe more formidable than any external enemy.

In this story, set against the grim backdrop of a battlefield, the visceral struggle for survival converges with an internal pilgrimage, seeking the Zen understanding of ego. Prepare yourself for an exploration of self, as raw as the battlefield, as complex as the labyrinth of the mind.

Amid the guttural roars and clanging metal, Panda felt an eerie calm wash over him. His sword felt light in his hands, and he moved through the battlefield with a sense of clarity he had never known before. This was his moment, his mind told him, the climax of all his training and hardships. The ego swelled within him like an inflated balloon, ready to burst.

But then, a fleeting thought crept in: "What if I fail? What if, despite all my skills, I fall here, in this godforsaken place?" Doubt began to wrap around his heart like a vine, choking the confidence that had just blossomed. The ego deflated, retreating into a dark corner of his psyche. Now, his sword felt heavy, and his limbs sluggish.

Just as his resolve began to waver, Panda's eyes met those of a wounded soldier lying in the mud—a tiger with battle stripes that mirrored his own internal conflicts. In that moment, Panda found his middle path. Neither the braggart nor the cowardly retreat of ego would serve him here. The tiger, despite his condition, nodded as if sharing an unspoken understanding.

Refocused and re-energized, Panda moved through the rest of the battle like water flowing down a stream, neither hurried nor sluggish, neither overconfident nor underprepared. He fought not to prove anything to himself or others but because, in that moment, it was the action that required his full presence.

When the dust settled, and the sounds of war faded into an unsettling silence, Panda sat down, breathing heavily. His body was exhausted, but his spirit felt light. He had faced many enemies on the battlefield that day, but the most formidable had been his own ego, and it was an enemy he realized he would face again and again on the path of life. But armed with the wisdom of balance—the Middle Way— he felt ready for whatever would come next.

As he walked away from the battlefield, the wounded tiger looked up. This time, Panda nodded back, acknowledging the unspoken pact that they would both continue to fight their internal battles, as much as the external ones, in pursuit of a deeper understanding and, ultimately, inner peace.

Chapter 29: The Illusion of Control

In a place where the whispers of ancient wisdom meld with the echoes of silent contemplation, there is an invitation— not just to observe but to partake in a secret dance of reality and illusion. Monastery walls, you think? Ah, more like porous membranes separating the folly of human control from the humble acceptance of life's flow. Here, the monks are not just keepers of secrets but students of the sublime art of letting go.

A young monk sits in a corner, wrapped in his own thoughts like a caterpillar in a cocoon. He's always believed that if he were strict enough with his practice, he could avoid the suffering that haunts the human condition. Today, however, he's received news from the outside world that his childhood friend has passed away. A tidal wave of grief engulfs him, and for a moment, he's drowning, grasping for a lifeline.

His eyes flit to the elder monk, who appears as serene as a still pond. The elder monk picks up a clay pot filled with water and pours it onto a small tree planted in the middle of the courtyard. Yet, for every drop that nourishes the tree, some evaporate into the air, never to return. The elder doesn't chase the evaporating drops or lament their loss; he simply continues his act of watering.

In this simple act, the young monk glimpses the truth: Control is a mirage in the desert of existence. The elder monk can nourish the tree but can't command every drop to do his bidding. Likewise, no amount of piety or practice can fully exempt one from life's inbuilt quotient of sorrow.

There is no escaping the ebb and flow of joy and suffering, of love and loss. As this wisdom settles over him like dew on morning leaves, the young monk feels his internal tightness loosen. He finds himself joining the chant, his voice a newfound wave in an ancient ocean, adding depth to the collective understanding that suffering, uncontrollable and inevitable, is also a pathway to deeper awareness.

Chapter 30: The Unwatered Seed

A young fox hesitated at the edge of a clearing, doubting its ability to cross the open space without becoming prey. Finally, it shook off its indecision, darted across the clearing, and disappeared safely into the brush on the other side. There, it found a bounty of berries it would have missed had doubt kept it paralyzed.

Final Thought: The seed of doubt only grows if you water it. Sometimes, the bravest thing you can do is let that seed wither—clearing the soil for confidence to bloom.

PART IV:
Realise Your Ultimate Potential

Chapter 31: The Forgotten Pages

"Here, between ink and parchment, resides my sanctuary a forest of thoughts, a river of reflections, a mountain of uncertainties. Yet, as I etch my existence into these blank canvases, they transform into stepping stones, guiding me toward something that feels a lot like potential, but also a lot like chaos. Today, I commence a journey without movement, a pilgrimage without shrines. Call it what you may—self-discovery, the search for wisdom, the realization of purpose—I call it 'becoming.'

If these pages could speak, they would whisper secrets not yet known to me. They are blank but far from empty; like my path ahead, they are imbued with possibilities too varied to predict and too vast to control. Perhaps you, dear reader, will find fragments of yourself scattered in my musings. And as you wander through my textual maze, may you find not answers, but better questions; not certainty, but a more comfortable abode in the unknown. Because here, in the labyrinth of life, getting lost is the first step in being found.

Welcome to my diary, the map of a terrain yet to be explored, the prologue to a story not yet written. We begin."

Chapter 32: Limitless Becoming

Today, I find myself sitting cross-legged under the ancient Wisdom Tree, its leaves rustling like whispered secrets from the universe. This old friend of mine has heard more confessions than any monk in the temple. Its roots, like gnarled hands, have embraced the dirt and mud to find sustenance, teaching me that from humble beginnings come great things.

Ah, potential. The word feels like a firefly in a jar captivating but restless, eager to break free. I recall the younger me, still unsure how to balance bamboo shoots on his nose, tumbling more often than not. How far I've come!

18th of the Bamboo Moon

Ran into Master Shunryū today. In a past life, we would have exchanged words, debated Zen koans until the moon claimed the sky. Now, a knowing glance suffices. In that glance, all my trials, tribulations, and triumphs seemed to have been acknowledged. He knows, as do I, that realizing one's potential is not the end but a beginning of another quest—perhaps a never-ending one.

22nd of the Bamboo Moon

Today, no new lessons, no grand teachings. Just a moment with myself, a cup of green tea, and the quietude that comes with being present. It struck me then, sipping my tea, how every gulp was a testament to the years of trials and errors, failures and triumphs. My potential wasn't a thing to be reached but a process to be lived, every day.

28th of the Bamboo Moon

I looked at the night sky. The stars seemed to wink back, as if confirming a secret we both knew but never talked about. We're all made of stardust, infinitely connected to each other and the universe. My potential, then, is not just mine but a part of a larger tapestry, interwoven with the fate and fortunes of others. A humbling yet empowering thought.

Panda Note: Dear readers, this book is not a path but a paving stone. Your potential isn't waiting at the end of the road; it's found in each step you take. Cherish the journey, for it is in walking that we find our way. And remember, even a thousand-mile journey starts with a single paw step.

Chapter 33: Unveiled Potential

15th of the Cherry Blossom Moon

The monks often say that the river never crosses the same mountain twice. Is it the same with potential? Does it reshape itself with each new moon? I've been sitting on this mat, watching the bamboo sway for countless cycles. Yet, each time it's as if I am seeing them for the first time. Fresh. New. What does that say about potential, or about me?

17th of the Cherry Blossom Moon

Today, Master Wu mentioned the lotus, perfect in its imperfections, constantly reaching towards the light but rooted in the mud. It made me ponder—am I any different? I have always been content munching bamboo, but is that my lotus? Or is the mud I'm rooted in restraining my potential? Ah, paradoxes are never far in this place.

19th of the Bamboo Moon

I observed a leaf today, crisply outlined against the sky. It looked simple yet complex, much like the nature of being. I wonder, does the leaf know its role in the grand scheme? Or does it simply exist? My thoughts wander to my own existence. The complexity of our simple lives, a web weaved by the threads of fate and choice, making us who we are. But is this all? Is there not more to glean, to become?

30th of the Cherry Blossom Moon

Today, I experienced something extraordinary during meditation. There was no forest, no bamboo, and no temple—just an infinite expanse of clear sky stretching as far as the eye could see. In that space, I felt lighter than ever, as if the weight of all my former concerns and limited beliefs had been lifted.

It struck me then: this limitless sky was a mirror to my own potential, boundless and unending. All the arbitrary boundaries I had set for myself seemed trivial, like clouds that momentarily block the sun but can never dim its light.

There's a newfound freedom in this revelation, a soaring realization that comes from recognizing the endless sky within. And so, I resolve to live each day with this expansive understanding, letting my potential unfurl like a sky without horizon.

Final Thought: Sometimes, the walls confining us exist only in the mind. When those walls come down, what's left is the sky.

Chapter 34: Luck – Action - Reaction

8th of the Moonbeam

I ventured into the heart of the city today, where skyscrapers kiss the heavens and ambitions run high. The energy was electrifying, a concrete jungle echoing with the footsteps of seekers—seekers of success, love, happiness. My focus was drawn to two young entrepreneurs, both in adjacent offices but worlds apart in their approach to life.

The first sat in his room, browsing through websites and social media, occasionally sighing as he glanced at the empty email inbox on his computer screen. His startup was at a standstill, as if waiting for some magic twist of fate to set things in motion. "Luck isn't on my side," he'd often murmur to himself, lamenting his stalled dreams.

Just a wall away, his neighbour, an equally young but far more animated man, was on constant calls, scribbling plans on whiteboards, and stepping out to meet potential clients. Every rejection was met with a pivot, a readjustment of strategy, a renewed energy for the next pitch. "Each 'no' is a step closer to a 'yes'," he'd say.

At the close of the day, the active entrepreneur received an email confirming a new contract. Jubilant, he looked out his window to catch the sunset, thinking how fortunate he was. But was it luck? He had cast so many stones into the pond; it was inevitable that ripples would eventually come back to him.

Some wait for the wheel of fortune to spin in their favour, ignoring the fact that they have the power to spin it themselves. It's not just luck, but the courage to take action that creates a reaction, echoing back as opportunities we often credit to good fortune. In the dance of life, action invites luck to take the floor.

Chapter 35: Zazen and Mindfulness

8th of the Moon of the Cascading Water

Today was unlike any other; it was a day enveloped in the ancient practice of Zazen. I found myself perched on a wooden stool overlooking the Sacred Falls—its water cascading endlessly, just as my thoughts often do. Master Wu had often mentioned that Zazen was less about 'doing' and more about 'being.'

As I sat there, my back erect, paws folded, and eyes half-closed, I tuned in to the subtle dance of existence around me. The distant calls of the mountain birds, the soft rustle of the autumn leaves, and the perpetual tumble of the waterfall formed a serene symphony.

I drew my attention inward, focusing on my breath—just my breath—as if each inhale and exhale was a rare treasure. Then it occurred to me: Zazen isn't merely an act; it's a state of mindful being. I wasn't just observing the breath; I was the breath, the air flowing through me, linking me with the surrounding world in an intimate embrace.

Slowly, I began to realize how each moment encapsulated its universe of potentiality. How often had I glossed over the little things? How frequently had I missed the hidden beauties, submerged in thoughts and fantasies? Each moment I had lost was a missed brushstroke on the canvas of life, a note missing from my life's song.

12th of the Moon of the Cascading Water

My paws met the parchment today as if for the first time. Each stroke felt more deliberate, every curve a testament to the newfound mindfulness. It wasn't a hurried act of writing but a careful expression of what was blossoming within. Every word seemed infused with potential, each pause a meditative space where thoughts could bloom or wither, unfettered by judgment.

Through Zazen and mindfulness, I've understood the vastness of the present. In that vastness, I have found the cradle of all potential, where every thought and every act are born not out of compulsion but from a profound engagement with the 'now.' There's a unique kind of freedom here—a liberation not from the world but within it.

The act of being, I've discovered, is the greatest testament to potential. After all, how can we realize what is possible if we're not fully present to sense it, touch it, and embrace it? The present moment is not a fleeting passage to the next experience; it's the grand stage upon which the performance of potential unfolds.

In these moments of stillness, I sense an expansiveness, like the boundless sky above or the deep, nurturing earth below. Each thought, each breath, each sensation becomes an echo of what's possible, a whisper of untapped potential, awaiting the light of mindful awareness to fully bloom

Chapter 36: Mindful Alchemy

Date: Moon of the Crimson Phoenix 8

Today I crossed paths with a wandering alchemist, a peculiar man encased in layers of ink-stained robes. He spent his days not just mixing herbs or turning lead into gold, but delving into the alchemy of the mind and soul.

Date: Moon of the Crimson Phoenix

The alchemist showed me an array of jars filled with dark, murky liquids. "These," he said, "are memories and feelings trapped in form. Each jar contains a negative experience or emotion."

Date: Moon of the Crimson Phoenix 10

He selected a jar labelled 'Anguish' and began to pour its contents into a complex array of tubes and cauldrons. A noxious fume arose, but he chanted incantations and applied flame beneath the cauldron. Slowly, the liquid changed, the fumes dissipated, and what remained was an entirely different substance—clear as crystal, with a mesmerizing glow.

Date: Moon of the Crimson Phoenix 12

"Transmutation," he said. "The key to Mindful Alchemy. We can't avoid suffering, but we can change what we do with it. We can turn our anguish into wisdom, our fears into courage and our sorrow into compassion."

Date: Moon of the Crimson Phoenix 16

I watched the alchemist practice his art, and I realized that this is the path I've been on. I, too, have a cauldron within me, a vessel where experiences mingle and combine. It's easy to let the brew turn toxic, to let pain fester into bitterness or confusion. But it's also possible to transmute that raw emotion into something nobler. Into insight. Into a greater capacity to love. Into a deeper appreciation for the very struggles that test our mettle.

Date: Moon of the Crimson Phoenix 20

As I walked away from the alchemist, his parting words reverberated in my ears, "Your life is the greatest alchemy. Every moment you live, every hurdle you cross, you're refining your essence, improving your formula, learning to transmute the base into the divine."

My path isn't just about reaching some mythical end point of 'ultimate potential.' It's about constantly refining, constantly transmuting, until the substance of my very being is imbued with wisdom, compassion, and unshakeable peace.

Chapter 37: Infinite Circles of Awareness

Date: Fiery Sky Moon 5

Today I found myself at the edge of the monastery's pond. It's a place I frequent, but today was different. As I stared into the water, each ripple seemed to resonate with a truth I had never considered. As the circles expanded, so did my thoughts.

Date: Fiery Sky Moon 7

While meditating in the hall, a realization hit me. What if enlightenment isn't a point but a circle? Not a peak that stands aloof, but a contour ever-expanding? The less I sought to 'reach' somewhere, the more infinite my possibilities became. I felt my awareness moving, not upward, but outward, like the ripples in the pond.

Date: Fiery Sky Moon 12

Master Wu shared an ancient parable today. The tale spoke of a monk who wanted to find the centre of the universe. He travelled to sacred sites, climbed towering mountains, and crossed expansive deserts. Exhausted, he returned only to find that the centre was where he started: within himself. That got me thinking. Maybe my potential isn't something 'out there.' It's right here, an ever-widening circle with no centre or circumference.

Date: Fiery Sky Moon 15

During Zazen, I usually focus on my breath. But today, I let my awareness fan out in all directions. I sensed the rustle of leaves, the distant murmur of the river, and even the slow crawl of a snail on the temple floor. And as my awareness expanded, so did my sense of self. It was as if I was part of a cosmic symphony, a player in the Infinite Orchestra, contributing my unique note to the universal melody.

Date: Fiery Sky Moon 21

The monastery held a festival today, and I was in charge of drawing the labyrinth for the walking meditation. As I etched each circle within a circle, I recognized my own path reflected in the spirals. Each revolution a different lifetime, each curve a different lesson. The labyrinth became a mirror, and as others walked it, their journey became a part of my own ever-expanding circle.

Date: Fiery Sky Moon 26

I ventured out to the cliff that overlooks the valley today. As I watched the sun dip below the horizon, painting the sky with strokes of orange and purple, a profound peace enveloped me. It felt as if the world and I were in a quiet dialogue, and the essence of it all was simply this: be.

I've come to see that my potential is not a peak waiting to be scaled but a circle ever-widening. The road to becoming is not a line; it's a spiral, ever-turning and expansive. With each Cosmic Spiral, I continue to multiply my possibilities and broaden my scope, understanding that the path doesn't end; it only widens, embracing everything in its eternal dance.

Chapter 38: The Unseen Orchestra

Date: Harmony Wind Moon 8

In the soft embrace of twilight, the forest came alive in whispers. Crickets initiated the first movement, a rhythmic undercurrent that flowed like a meandering river through the underbrush. Not far off, the cicadas joined, their sonorous timbre mingling with the wind's gentle sighs.

Date: Harmony Wind Moon 12

The moon ascended, and with it rose the melody of the nightingales, notes embroidered onto the fabric of the night. Their song reverberated through the leaves, a poetic call resonating in the open air, filling the gaps between the branches and the stars.

Date: Harmony Wind Moon 16

Above, constellations twinkled, each a silent chord in a celestial symphony. Unseen but felt, the gravitational pull they exerted on Earth was like a bow caressing the strings of a violin—subtle yet profound.

Date: Harmony Wind Moon 20

Closer to home, the rustle of bamboo leaves played counterpoint to the chorus of the brook. Water over stones, a repetitive theme, each droplet a different note but part of the same melody. Together, they produced a harmonious tapestry that felt ancient and yet ever-new.

Date: Harmony Wind Moon 26

I sat there, silent yet listening, separate yet connected. My fur felt the subtle air currents, my paws sensed the vitality of the earth, my ears caught the nuanced orchestrations of life's grand symphony. In that moment, it became clear that my own existence, my own potential, was but a note in this complex arrangement of the universe.

Date: Harmony Wind Moon 30

As dawn broke, the first rays of light infused the sky with colour, the grand finale in a concert that had spanned the night. The forest awoke in stretches and yawns, each creature, each element taking a bow, grateful for the role they played in the masterpiece that had unfolded.

In this orchestra where every leaf, every feather, every star is an instrument, there are no rehearsals—only live performances. To participate fully is to be in tune, not just with the self but with the unseen, the grand ensemble that plays the eternal composition of existence.

Chapter 39: Training Ground

Date: Autumn Moon 21

Today, I observed athletes at a training ground. A place pulsating with relentless energy and purpose. Amidst hurdles and tracks, humans stretched the boundaries of their physical capacities.

Date: Autumn Moon 22

One athlete in particular caught my eye. He didn't clear the hurdle gracefully; instead, he knocked it down. The clatter seemed to echo across the field.

Date: Autumn Moon 23

The same athlete set the hurdle upright once more, took a deep breath, and launched himself again. This time he cleared it, not with grace, but with gritty determination. The victory was in his stance, a promise of potential realized not in perfection but in persistence.

Date: Autumn Moon 24

The sun began to set, casting a golden glow over the field. As the athletes packed up, a new kind of energy stirred within me. It's not the hurdles we face, but the courage to set them upright and try again that defines our ultimate potential.

Chapter 40: Gym

Date: Snowfall Moon 12

Today, I wandered into an area of the forest where the animals have devised their own makeshift training grounds. It wasn't exactly a gym, but it had the air of one logs to be lifted, vines to be swung, boulders to be rolled.

Date: Snowfall Moon 14

Chu, the elephant, was using his trunk to lift a massive tree trunk. I could see the sheer determination in his eyes, a living testament to raw strength refined over time. It made me think about my own untapped potential, not just in physical strength but in mastering the art of being.

Date: Snowfall Moon 16

I noticed Lin, the rabbit, darting from one corner to the other with remarkable speed. He wasn't as strong as Chu, but his agility was unparalleled. I wondered, could strength manifest in different forms? Could I be strong in my own unique way?

Date: Snowfall Moon 18

Something curious caught my attention today. Ying, the turtle, slowly but steadily pushing a round boulder up a slope. His movements were deliberate, and his progress was slow, but he never stopped. It dawned on me that sometimes the path to unlocking potential is neither fast nor flashy, but persistent.

Date: Snowfall Moon 20

As I meditated on a rock, it hit me: the idea of physical prowess is a form of potential, but it's just the tip of the iceberg. Chu's strength, Lin's agility, Ying's persistence—they were all channels for a deeper, more expansive understanding. An understanding that every choice we make—whether to lift or to run or to persist—brings us closer to our fullest expression.

Moreover, unlocking one's potential isn't just about achieving physical prowess or reaching a specific milestone; it's about continually expanding one's understanding of what they are capable of.

PART V:
In a World of Chaos

Chapter 41: Social Media Overwhelm

Subject: Lost in the Maze
From: Panda
To: ZenMasterEagle

Dear ZenMasterEagle,
I always wander aimlessly in the Infinite Maze of Talking Statues. Each statue bombards me with information—some poetic, some philosophical, some completely nonsensical. It's like being inside the internet, but worse. I can't seem to find peace. Help!

Best, Panda.

Subject: The Way Out is In
From: ZenMasterEagle
To: Panda

Dear Panda,
You're lost in the labyrinth of life, entangled in voices and choices. It's easy to get lost out there. But the true way out? It's within you. Close your eyes. Breathe. Focus only on your breath. Let the chatter become background noise. Soon, you'll find a silence so profound, it's like you've become the maze itself. And in that silence, your path will become clear.

Yours in tranquillity, ZenMasterEagle.

Panda read the email and did as advised. He closed his eyes, took deep breaths, and suddenly, the maze seemed less daunting. It was as if the walls became transparent, and he could see a path.

He walked, following the clarity he felt, until he reached the centre of the maze. There, he found no statue but a simple Zen garden—a perfect square of raked sand. He knew he had found his way.

Taking out his phone, he logged back into his social media accounts. This time, it was different. The noise didn't overwhelm him. Instead, he navigated through it, calmly and wisely, interacting only with what truly mattered.

And so, Panda learned to navigate the chaotic, intricate web of modern existence without losing his peace, finding enlightenment in the labyrinth of life.

Chapter 42: Environmental Crisis

Panda was bobbing along the endless blue horizon, surrounded by floating bamboo huts and repurposed plastic platforms. The Eco-Village was like an island, yet unlike any other—alive, always moving, and sustained entirely by its eco-conscious inhabitants.

As Panda admired the ingenuity of the floating village, he was approached by a dolphin named Luna, the village's informal leader.

Luna: "Welcome, Panda! You look impressed. Not what you expected from a community floating on garbage, eh?"

Panda: "Indeed, Luna. I can't help but wonder how you manage to turn waste into something so beautiful and functional."

Luna: "Ah, but that's the secret, Isn't it? Seeing value where others see waste. What brings you to our drifting haven?"

Panda: "I've been observing the destructive force of climate change back home. The bamboo forests are wilting, the rivers are polluted. It's a mess. But what can one panda do?"

Luna: "Ah, the paralysis of insignificance. It plagues many. But tell me, Panda, what does Zen teach about action?"

Panda: "Compassionate action. Acting not because you must, but because your innate compassion leaves you no other option."

Luna: "Exactly! You see, each one of us contributes in small ways. I guide schools of fish away from polluted areas. Stella, the seagull over there, helps in cleaning micro plastics from the surface of the water. Each small act is a ripple that turns into a wave."

Panda: "So, it's not about the scale of the action, but the quality of intention behind it."

Luna: "You've got it, Panda. Compassionate action has a way of multiplying its impact in ways we can't even fathom."

Panda: "Thank you, Luna. I needed this enlightenment. I'll return to my forest and do what I can, with the resources I have. Every bamboo I plant, every river I help clean, will be an act of compassion, not just for me but for the Earth."

Luna: "And that's how change happens, Panda—one compassionate act at a time."

As Panda bid farewell to Luna and the remarkable Floating Eco-Village, he felt a newfound sense of purpose. For the first time, the environmental crisis seemed neither distant nor insurmountable. And as he set sail back to his wilting bamboo forest, he knew he carried with him the seeds of change, sown in the soil of compassionate action.

Chapter 43: Political Unrest

The heart of the Quicksand Coliseum, a grand arena whose floor was a living, ever-changing arras of quicksand that responds to the crowd's emotions.

The crowd roared. To his left were the Blues, shouting for justice and equality. To his right were the Reds, crying for tradition and order. The quicksand beneath him twisted and turned, as if trying to pull him into its depths.

"But what if neither side has all the answers?" Panda pondered aloud. The crowd paused, and for a moment, the quicksand seemed to hesitate. "What if the Middle Way—considering perspectives from both sides—leads to the most balanced and rational viewpoint?"

The crowd roared again. Reds and Blues yelled, each believing their side was right. Yet, a few in the audience, from both sides, began to nod thoughtfully. The quicksand slowed its relentless twisting.

As Panda stood in the centre of the Coliseum, he felt the ground beneath him solidify. The crowd, once a cacophony of opposing views, fell into a thoughtful silence. Panda knew that he had found his answer: the Middle Way. And in doing so, he had brought a momentary balance to the ever-changing sands of the Quicksand Coliseum.

In a world constantly pulling him towards one extreme or another, Panda had found his balance by embracing the wisdom of the Middle Way. The audience may not have wholly changed their views, but the sands of the Coliseum stood still, if only for a brief moment, reflecting the equilibrium that comes from a balanced perspective.
Panda found himself in the heart of the Quicksand Coliseum, a grand arena whose floor was a living, ever-changing tapestry of quicksand that responded to the crowd's emotions.

The crowd roared. To his left were the Blues, shouting for justice and equality. To his right were the Reds, crying for tradition and order. The quicksand beneath him twisted and turned, as if trying to pull him into its depths.

"But what if neither side has all the answers?" Panda pondered aloud. The crowd paused, and for a moment, the quicksand seemed to hesitate. "What if the Middle Way—considering perspectives from both sides—leads to the most balanced and rational viewpoint?"

The crowd roared again. Reds and Blues yelled, each believing their side was right. Yet, a few in the audience, from both sides, began to nod thoughtfully. The quicksand slowed its relentless twisting.

As Panda stood in the centre of the Coliseum, he felt the ground beneath him solidify. The crowd, once a cacophony of opposing views, fell into a thoughtful silence. Panda knew that he had found his answer: the Middle Way. And in doing so, he had brought a momentary balance to the ever-changing sands of the Quicksand Coliseum.

In a world constantly pulling him towards one extreme or another, Panda had found his balance by embracing the wisdom of the Middle Way. The audience may not have wholly changed their views, but the sands of the Coliseum stood still, if only for a brief moment, reflecting the equilibrium that comes from a balanced perspective.

Chapter 44: Work-Related Stress

Day like any other, Panda's paws pounding on the keyboard, each keystroke resounding through the office like the ticks of a colossal clock. Wheels, cogs, and gears adorning the walls, turning in time with the frantic pace of work. His deadline is approaching and the clockwork mechanisms seem to mock him with their perfectly timed rotations.

"Tick-tock, Panda, the report won't write itself," his boss, Mr. Rhino, bellowed from his open door, which itself rotated like the hands of a clock, making it hard to distinguish when he was actually in the office or out.

Panda sighed, his gaze stuck between the screen and the ever-turning cogs on the wall. Anxiety gnawed at him. What if he failed? What if he succeeded but the success meant more work, more stress?

Suddenly, a Zen teaching flashed in his mind: Detachment from Outcomes. It was like a cog fitting into place, altering the entire machinery of his perspective. He realized he had been too attached to the fear of failure and the pressure of success.

He closed his eyes for a moment and took a deep breath, refocusing. When he opened them again, the room seemed the same but felt different. The gears and cogs were just gears and cogs, not tormentors ticking away his time or joy.

With renewed vigour, Panda returned to his report. He tapped the keys not as a desperate attempt to beat time but as an act of being fully in the present, detaching himself from the outcomes. Each word he wrote became not a tick closer to deadline doom but a tock closer to personal fulfilment.

Finally, Panda hit the "Send" button. As if in acknowledgment, the clockwork walls seemed to pause briefly in their rotations. Mr. Rhino peeked out from his rotating door, a smile widening on his face.

"Excellent work, Panda," he said. But Panda simply nodded, appreciating the compliment but not becoming attached to it.

As he left the office, which now seemed less like a ticking trap and more like an intricate ballet of time and effort, Panda felt lighter than he had ever felt. He had not just completed a task; he had experienced it fully, without the shackles of fear or expectation. And for the first time, the tick-tocking around him sounded not like a countdown to stress but like the rhythmic beating of a peaceful heart.

In navigating the chaos of the Clockwork Office, Panda found tranquillity by detaching himself from outcomes, turning each tick and tock into a moment of Zen.

Chapter 45: Consume Culture

Panda sauntered through the bustling aisles of the Market of Ephemeral Wonders, his eyes widening at each stall. Vendors sold bottled laughter, canned sunsets, and sachets of silence. Advertisements buzzed in the air, a kaleidoscope of colours and sounds promising eternal happiness with each purchase.

"Step right up, step right up!" A vendor with a top hat and a sparkle in his eyes caught Panda's attention. "Buy some Time! Never enough of it, am I right?"

Panda pondered. Time seemed like a wonderful thing to have more of. Just then, another stall caught his eye. "Joy in a Jar! Get your unlimited happiness right here!"

His paw hovered hesitantly over his wallet. That's when the Zen teaching echoed in his mind: Embrace Impermanence. He looked around the market, at the faces clutching their newly bought 'Eternal Youths' and 'Forever Loves,' and he saw not joy but a perpetual hunger for more.

With a polite nod to the vendors, Panda turned and left the market, empty-pawed but not empty-hearted. He recognized the beauty in the transience of his experiences—the uncatchable laughter, the sunsets that slipped away, the silence that always gave way to a new sound. For the first time, he felt the weight of the constant consumerism lift off his shoulders.

As he strolled away, he felt the wind brush against his fur and heard the rustle of bamboo leaves in the distance. The world seemed vibrant, full of fleeting moments that were here and then gone, leaving room for new experiences to come.

In not buying into the illusion of permanence sold at the Market of Ephemeral Wonders, Panda found a contentment that was as enduring as it was ever-changing. It was a curious transaction, one where not buying anything gave him everything he really needed.

And so, Panda continued on his way, richer in his understanding that the most precious things in life aren't things at all.

Chapter 46: Relationship Troubles

Panda stepped into the Mystic Room of Mirrors with hesitant curiosity. Each mirror was framed in intricately carved wood and seemed to glow with an inner light. He had heard tales that this room could reveal the truth of one's relationships, not just with others but also with oneself.

Panda approached the first mirror, and his reflection began to speak. "Why are you always so busy? Why don't you listen?" it questioned.

Remembering the lesson of Mindfulness in Communication, Panda took a deep breath and focused his entire being on the mirror. "I'm here now, completely present. What would you like to tell me?"

His reflection smiled. "Just that, sometimes, silence and presence are all a relationship needs."

Walking to the second mirror, Panda found himself staring at an image of him and his forest friends, each one turning into someone more "ideal" and less like themselves. Recalling the teaching of Detachment from Expectations, Panda whispered, "You are enough as you are," and watched as the reflections morphed back to their true selves.

The third mirror presented an unsettling sight. Panda and his closest friend, Bunny, were in a heated argument. Remembering the value of Compassion over Conflict, Panda spoke softly to his reflection: "What pain are you feeling that makes you act this way?" His reflected self paused, softening, a subtle nod acknowledging the wisdom in this compassionate approach.

In the fourth mirror, Panda saw himself standing alone at the edge of the forest while his friends were huddled together. It reminded him of the Middle Way in Commitment. "I can be part of the group while also finding time for myself," he mused, watching his reflection walk back to join his friends but also carrying a book, a symbol of his own interests and identity.

The final mirror showed Panda as a young cub, then as an old bear, and all ages in between. Panda sighed, contemplating the impermanence of it all. Then, realizing Impermanence as a Strength, he smiled, "Each phase has its own beauty and challenges. Each moment is a new relationship waiting to happen."

As Panda exited the room, he felt a profound sense of tranquillity. He knew he had relationships to mend and friendships to cherish, but armed with these lessons, he felt better equipped to face them. The Mystic Room of Mirrors had shown him not just his reflections but the wisdom of relational existence. From that day on, Panda navigated his relationships with a sense of enlightenment, understanding that every interaction was a mirror, a teacher, and a lesson rolled into one.

Chapter 47: Personal Illness or Injury

Panda had heard tales of the Healing Caves, a place where luminescent walls held mysterious restorative powers. Eager to ease his discomfort, Panda set off on a journey to find the fabled caves.

Upon entering the cave, the soft glow of the luminescent walls seemed to greet him. Deep within, he discovered an inscription that read, "To heal the body, first understand the mind." This message made him pause. He realized that his suffering had consumed his thoughts, casting a shadow over his entire life.

Determined to understand the teaching, Panda continued exploring and soon found a chamber with a glowing pool at its centre. He dipped his sore paw into the water, expecting immediate relief. Though the water was soothing, his paw continued to ache.

It was then that Panda remembered the Zen teaching to accept suffering as a part of life's natural course. Embracing this wisdom, he felt a mental burden lift, as if the walls of the cave acknowledged his newfound understanding by glowing even brighter.

Taking his paw out of the water, he discovered that although the swelling had not disappeared, the weight of his suffering felt significantly lighter. As he exited the cave, it seemed as though the luminescence dimmed momentarily, bidding him a soft farewell.

Back in his forest, Panda continued to limp but with a different air about him. The pain was still present, but it no longer dominated his thoughts. Through his journey into the Healing Caves, Panda hadn't just sought physical relief; he had gained a deep, enriching understanding of life's natural cycles of joy and suffering—and the peace that comes from accepting both.

Chapter 48: Family Responsibilities

It was a dimension where architecture breathed, the Living Homestead adapted and evolved with the moods and milestones of its ever-changing inhabitants.

Panda, who had many responsibilities in taking care of this dynamic home, was overwhelmed. Between feeding the "kitchen" that digested compost, soothing the "living room" that sometimes got too lively, and tuning the "study" that grew smarter by the day, he was exhausted. His younger siblings ran around, playing tag and hide-and-seek with the rooms themselves. And amidst all this, the walls of the house would contract and expand like a breathing organism.

However, one day, Panda discovered a room he had never noticed before: a serene chamber filled with the aroma of incense and the gentle sound of a running stream. The room seemed to invite him in for a moment of quiet contemplation. Panda entered, sitting in the centre of the room, closing his eyes.

As he inhaled and exhaled, following the principles of mindful breathing inspired by Buddhist teachings, he felt the chaos from the rest of the home start to fade away. Within the silence, he found the answer to his overwhelming responsibilities. It was not the house that needed to be managed but his reaction to it. The key lay in finding tranquillity amid the chaos, the 'Sound of Silence.'

When he opened his eyes, the room had transformed into a mini-sanctuary, mirroring his newfound inner peace. And as he returned to his duties, his actions flowed naturally, like water running its course. His family sensed the shift too; the whole Living Homestead became a little less boisterous, a little more harmonious.

From then on, Panda made it a point to visit the sanctuary room daily, practicing the art of embracing quiet within the noise, a lesson he would carry throughout his life, instilling a sense of serenity that could not be disturbed by the ever-changing dynamics of family life.

Chapter 49: Commuting Chaos

Once upon a traffic jam in the heart of Panda City, our hero Panda found himself in an unusual conundrum. His bamboo-mobile was caught in what could only be described as a fur-pulling, snout-snorting, utterly unbearable standstill. Around him, the frustrations were reaching a boiling point. One vehicle even had a cartoonish cloud of anger puffing out of its exhaust pipe.

"I can't bear this! I have places to go, bamboo to eat!" grumbled a disgruntled raccoon in the car next to Panda.

Panda, however, took a deep breath and started practicing mindfulness. "Ah, anger, my old friend. Thank you for visiting," he said to himself, identifying the emotion before it could take root.

"You talking to me?" asked a startled squirrel in roller skates zigzagging through the cars.

"No, my furry friend. Just making peace with my inner road rage."

The raccoon rolled his eyes, "Peace? Good luck with that!"

Panda smiled and began to channel Metta, or loving-kindness. "May I be happy, may I be peaceful," he started, before extending his wishes to everyone stuck in the traffic jam. "May the raccoon find his calm, may the squirrel not trip over a nut."

Just then, a flock of birds flying overhead decided to "drop" their frustrations on the cars below. The raccoon's car was splattered, and he was about to explode in a furry frenzy.

"ARGH! This is the worst day ever!"

Panda chuckled and calmly said, "Ah, the Middle Way. It's not the best day, but it's not the worst either. It just is."

With a puzzled expression, the raccoon hesitated, then asked, "Middle what now?"

"Equanimity, my friend. Finding balance in the imbalance. Like eating just enough bamboo to be full but not bloated."

Just then, the traffic began to move, as if the universe itself had found its balance. The raccoon looked at Panda and said, "You're a weird one, but I like you. What's your secret?"

Panda grinned from ear to fluffy ear, "Just a bit of ancient wisdom and a knack for seeing the humour in life."

As Panda rolled away, he couldn't help but feel a sense of peace envelop him. The raccoon, still puzzled but intrigued, started muttering to himself, "Middle Way, huh? Maybe I should try some of that bamboo diet."

And so, amidst the chaos of Panda City traffic, our hero found serenity, proving once again that even in the most infuriating circumstances, enlightenment is but a thought away.

Chapter 50: Public Outrage, Cancel Culture

Around the bustling corner of the mystical realm, hidden amidst the swirling galaxies and existential questions, lay a place known to all but entered by few: The Court of Public Opinion. It was an amphitheatre so grand and ancient that even the oldest of stars had tales of its dread. The Court was the epitome of dark humour, a place where one's fate could swing wildly between sainthood and villainy, often within a single cosmic heartbeat.

Panda, the ever-curious wanderer, found himself in this perilous arena. He looked around, and all he could see were faces, young and old, critters and creatures from all walks of life, holding enchanted devices that glowed and buzzed.

"Order! Order!" thundered the presiding Owl from a tall pedestal, her eyes magnified to ominous proportions by her circular spectacles. "We are gathered here today to pass judgment on Mr. Whiskers, who has been accused of—gasp—eating the last slice of cosmic pie!"

A murmur of shock rippled through the crowd. Panda couldn't believe it. Cosmic Pie was the equivalent of divine ambrosia in these parts, a pie so tasty it could make angels weep.

Before he knew it, the crowd was roaring. "Cancel him!" "Banish him to the Shadow Realm!" "Off with his whiskers!"

But Panda felt uneasy. "Wait a minute," he thought. "We all have our Buddha nature, our core of goodness and wisdom, don't we?"

Mustering courage, he stood up. "Uh, pardon the interruption, but has anyone thought about redemption or, you know, understanding why Mr. Whiskers ate the pie?"

The crowd gasped. The Owl raised an eyebrow.

Panda continued, "I mean, we all have the potential for both good and bad, right? Why not focus on understanding rather than condemning?"

For a moment, a silence swept over the Court. Then, a chuckle erupted from an old tortoise in the back, who was famous for his dry sense of humour. "Oh, look! We have a philosopher panda among us! What's next? Meditating for world peace?"

Panda chuckled. "Well, that wouldn't be a bad idea, would it?"

The Owl, amused yet intrigued, spoke, "Young Panda, you have a point. Let us adjourn this meeting to explore this...Buddha nature you speak of."

As the crowd dispersed, still puzzled but considerably less outraged, Panda found himself amidst an ocean of selfies and enchanted hashtags. #PandaWisdom started trending across the cosmic web.

He couldn't help but smile. "Ah, the absurdity and beauty of existence!" he mused, leaving the Court but taking a piece of its chaotic wisdom with him.

The Court of Public Opinion may be perilous, but as Panda showed, even in a universe ripe with judgments and quick conclusions, a little enlightenment goes a long way.

And so, amid dark humour and public outrage, our zen Panda found a fleeting moment of balance, a speck of light in the infinite dark canvas of public opinion.

PART VI:
Beyond the Meadow

Chapter 51: In a Realm of Pure Energy

In a realm of pure energy, oscillating between frequencies and vibrations that Panda could feel but not describe, he floated weightlessly. Here, there were no bamboo forests or streams, no Earth or Moon, just pulses of energy that communicated directly to his soul. A wave of radiant energy approached him, inviting him to sync with its frequency.

Feeling intrigued and adventurous, Panda matched his own vibrational pattern to that of the radiant energy. The moment he did, a surge of inspiration flowed through him, lighting up parts of his consciousness he never knew existed. The energy entity radiated a message: "You have accessed the Power Spectrum."

A lattice of radiant beams appeared before him, each representing different traits—courage, wisdom, love, among others. "Choose a beam and follow it," the energy entity encouraged.

Without hesitation, Panda chose the beam of courage. He felt himself propelled along it at an incredible speed, through colours and sounds he couldn't begin to describe. At the end of this exhilarating rush, a powerful realization dawned on him: courage wasn't a trait he lacked and needed to find; it was always within him, waiting to be activated.

Fully charged and invigorated, Panda suddenly found himself back in his world. But he wasn't the same Panda who had left. His steps now had a bold stride, and his actions felt surer, guided by an indomitable sense of courage.

He took on challenges he had never considered before, offering his own unique solutions. Whether helping a fellow animal out of a tricky situation or devising a new way to reach the tastiest bamboo shoots high up in the trees, Panda now approached everything with a level of courage and zest that not only surprised his friends but also himself.

The encounter in the realm of pure energy had not endowed him with new qualities but activated what was dormant within him. It was as if he had tuned into a frequency of himself that he never knew was broadcasting. And now that he had, there was no turning back. He had tasted the exhilarating freedom of living courageously, and he relished every moment of it, knowing he had tapped into a universal reservoir of strength that was always available, waiting for him to tune in.

Chapter 52: An Unanswerable Question

In a distant and dazzling citadel floating amidst an unending expanse of vibrant colours and luminescent gases, Panda found himself face-to-face with a being unlike any he had ever seen. It was a luminous, shape-shifting entity that defied all description—constantly changing in form, size, and hue.

"Welcome, Panda," it greeted, its voice a melodious symphony. "You have ventured beyond the boundaries of known spirituality, even beyond Buddhism. Do you dare ponder the unanswerable?"

Intrigued and slightly uneasy, Panda nodded. "I am ready."

"Then ponder this: What is the sound of one hand clapping?" The entity's voice trailed off into an ethereal echo, and the space around them seemed to hum in anticipation.

Panda's eyes widened. He was familiar with this Zen riddle, but the being shook its form in what seemed like amusement. "Ah, but here, that question has a different connotation, one that neither Zen nor any earthly philosophy can answer."

And then, as if the question had been a key, the citadel around them began to shift, each room transforming into a different puzzle, paradox, or conundrum. The walls themselves seemed to be formed of questions, posed in letters of fire, water, earth, and wind.

Just as Panda thought he might become overwhelmed, the being spoke again, "You see, each question here is a doorway, a cliff-hanger inviting you to explore further. But beware: each answer only births a new question."

This was the first cliff-hanger, and Panda felt a twinge of excitement and trepidation. "Then let me walk through this door. What is the answer to the question you posed?"

The being shimmered, its form splintering into a thousand different shapes before coalescing again. "The answer is that there is no answer, not here. The point is to ponder, to seek, to question. Understanding that concept is the first step in a journey with no end."

And as it spoke, another doorway appeared, leading to another unanswerable question, another cliff-hanger. "Does reality exist when you're not observing it?"

Panda's mind raced. "So, the journey itself is the destination?"

"Exactly," the being said, its form now turning into something resembling a cosmic swirl. "Are you ready for the next question, the next cliff-hanger?"

Panda nodded, feeling a newfound sense of enthusiasm. He had always sought answers, but now he realized that the real adventure lay in the questions themselves. Each one was a cliff-hanger, leading him on a never-ending journey of inquiry and wonder.

Feeling invigorated, he looked at the entity. "I am ready."

And so, with a question on his lips and an insatiable curiosity in his heart, Panda stepped through the new doorway, ready for the next unanswerable cliff-hanger, knowing that this journey had no end, but was filled with infinite fascinations. And somewhere deep within, he felt a thrill he had never known—the thrill of the eternal quest for the unanswerable.

Chapter 53: The Ethereal Chamber

In an ethereal chamber glowing with an indescribable light that seemed to resonate with the essence of all faiths, Panda felt both awed and puzzled. No bamboo here, no meditative streams—just a room adorned with sacred symbols from different traditions, each illuminating its corner in a unique radiance.

An old elephant approached, its skin etched with symbols from religions and philosophies around the world. "Welcome, young Panda, to the Chamber of Universal Wisdom," the elephant intoned. "Here, each faith sheds light on the same Eternal, just as each lamp in this room dispels its own share of darkness."

Panda felt his Buddhist teachings tingling at the back of his mind, sensing both accord and discord. "But how can all these paths lead to the same destination? Isn't that a contradiction?"

The elephant smiled gently. "Truth is like the sky. You can look at it from a mountaintop or a deep valley, during daylight or night-time, and it would appear different each time. Yet, it's still the same sky."

Panda reflected upon this, contemplating the wisdom he had gained from Buddhism and the new perspectives this chamber offered. He had an insight then—not a ground-breaking upheaval but a quiet understanding like a soft feather landing on still water.

"Could it be," mused Panda, "that my quest for enlightenment is like trying to capture the sky in a bamboo cup? Limiting yet limitless, specific yet universally applicable."

The elephant's eyes twinkled, "Ah, you begin to see. Inclusivity doesn't negate the uniqueness of your path, it enriches it."

In that pivotal moment, Panda felt as if the walls that had once confined his thoughts were not just dismantled but transformed into transparent pathways. It was a liberating awareness, the realization that wisdom could be multi-faceted and yet, remarkably, singular in its essence. With this newfound clarity, Panda felt neither tied to one creed nor isolated from others. Instead, he found himself at the crossroads of infinite possibilities, invigorated by the complex richness of it all.

Chapter 54: Beyond the Horizon

Panda: "Master, we spend our days steeped in the teachings of Buddhism, finding the path to enlightenment through its practices and principles. But is there a wisdom that exists beyond these teachings?"

Master: "Ah, you've opened a door to a room most are afraid to enter. Tell me, what makes you ask such a daring question?"

Panda: "I cannot help but wonder if our spiritual understanding is limited by the boundaries we set around it. The universe is infinitely complex; can one tradition hold all its answers?"

Master: "A river, no matter how wide, cannot contain the ocean. However, it can lead to it. Our teachings are the river. The ocean is what you seek—a wisdom that's not confined by words or teachings."

Panda: "So, the ocean is something experienced, not learned?"

Master: "Precisely. Just as you can describe water but must drink it to quench your thirst, so too you must experience this wisdom to truly know it."

Panda: "And how does one find this ocean, if it's beyond all maps?"

Master: "You must become a mapmaker. Each moment of true insight charts a course to a territory yet unexplored."

Panda: "A mapmaker in the realm of the unknown—I am intrigued and terrified at the same time."

Master: "As you should be. Mapmaking isn't for the faint of heart. It requires courage, for each new map could lead to treasure or treachery. But in the unknown, you will find the wisdom you seek, the wisdom that transcends all doctrine."

Panda: "So, to find what's beyond Buddhism, I must risk leaving its shores?"

Master: "Only by sailing into the open sea will you find new lands. But remember, when you set sail, don't forget the river that led you to the ocean. Buddhism is the vessel that has brought you this far; honour it, even as you search for more."

Panda: "I am grateful, Master, for this light you've shined on the path that extends beyond the horizon."

Master: "I haven't illuminated your path, my friend. I've only reminded you that you carry your own torch."

With a bow, Panda left the Master's presence, his mind swirling with possibilities, ready to become a mapmaker in realms yet uncharted.

Chapter 55: The Unknowable

Unfathomable. Unreachable. The corners of reality bending in ways that seem impossible. Lights that weren't lights flickered in shades of colours not found on any known spectrum. Was it a room? A space? A rift between what is and what can't be? Ah, the Panda enters. Why is it here? An echo answers, reverberating in structures of meaning that don't quite translate into words. It's not fear that grips Panda; it's sheer curiosity, mingled with a pinch of absurdity.

It stands on the precipice of understanding and not-understanding, teetering like an impossibly balanced stone.

"Unknowable," Panda muses, the concept stretching beyond its ability to grasp. What's the sound of one hand clapping? That's child's play. This was the cosmic question without a question mark, a riddle without words. Yet the Unknowable didn't feel menacing or cruel; it just was.

Panda sits, contemplating the indescribable. Its black and white fur shifts in patterns that mirror the flux around it. Ah, meditation, the old standby. But no, this is different. This isn't about finding answers or touching enlightenment. This is about being—being with what is not, what could be, and what can never be known.

And as if responding to this surrender to the great cosmic 'Is,' the room—or not-room—shifts. Not a shift in space or time, but a shift in the essence of what it means to be. The whispers grow silent. The not-lights dim. The Unknowable seems to bow, ever so slightly, acknowledging the humble wisdom of not-knowing.

Panda rises, and the incomprehensible space or not-space seems to open up, allowing exit or entrance or neither. It takes a step, leaving paw prints made of questions on the fabric of questions. And it exits, not back to where it came from, but back to a place that now seems richer, fuller for having touched the Unknowable.

Who's to say what Panda gained or lost? For how do you measure the weight of a question that can't be asked? But one thing's for sure: the cosmos winked, and Panda winked back. And that was enough.

Chapter 56: Nirvana

The sun's brilliant radiance surrounded Panda, enveloping him in a tapestry of intricate geometric patterns that danced and swirled in harmony. Each pulse of luminous energy seemed to resonate with his very being, unlocking visions of alien landscapes, vast civilizations stretching beyond comprehension, and ethereal realms teeming with life.

Within this kaleidoscopic maelstrom, Panda encountered entities, sentient manifestations of the sun's primal energy. They communicated not with words but with waves of emotion, guiding and comforting him. These beings, although alien in form, felt familiar, as if they were echoes of ancient wisdom residing deep within Panda's soul. As the sun's core drew nearer, the boundary between Panda and the universe began to blur. The realization hit him; he was experiencing a profound ego dissolution. The sense of "self", the ego that had accompanied him throughout his journey, started to fade, replaced by an overwhelming sensation of oneness with the cosmos.

The intensity of emotions surging through Panda was unlike anything he'd ever felt. Moments of pure euphoria intertwined with profound insights, occasionally punctuated by waves of fear, only to be replaced by deeper understanding and peace. Time, as he knew it, seemed to warp and twist. Moments felt like eons, and eons compressed into mere moments. This altered perception made Panda acutely aware of the eternal dance between the fleeting and the everlasting. And just as suddenly as it began, the experience started to wane. The visuals, entities, and intense emotions began to recede, gently lowering Panda back to his meditative state. Though he was once again grounded in familiar territory, the awe of his journey lingered, leaving him with a profound sense of enlightenment and connection to the universe.

PART VII:
Panda's Final Koan

Chapter 57: Oneness

Emerging from the silent corridors of deep meditation, a brilliant vision revealed to me the true essence of existence. Bathed in an endless cascade of love and peace, a sensation far removed from any worldly emotion I'd ever felt. Beliefs, traditions, cultures – they weave intricate patterns, but when beheld with a heart full of love, their differences blur. What remains is a singular, pulsating rhythm of unity. We often categorize and label, but perhaps these are just numerous paths leading us to the same profound truth of interconnectedness.

Every human is a kaleidoscope, a blend of light and shadow. Within this duality, there's a temptation to sway, to get lost. But authentic wisdom lies in recognizing this play and maintaining our balance, ensuring we remain grounded despite the dichotomous pulls of our being.

In this vast cosmos, every gesture, every whispered hope, has a ripple effect. Understanding this immense power, I implore you all to tread with consciousness, to treat every interaction as a sacred dance. For in every moment lies the potential to not only elevate our own spirit but to uplift others. Let us carry forth this anthem of universal love, recognizing that beneath varied guises, we all yearn for the same embrace of understanding and unity. Let our lives be a testament to this love, a beacon that reaffirms that at the heart of it all, love is our true nature.

ABOUT THE AUTHOR

Hiroto Takahashi, born in the serene town of Kamakura, was not just an ordinary Zen master; he was the epitome of enlightenment in the midst of mundane life. While most sought spiritual growth in the confines of temples, Hiroto found it in the bustling streets, crowded markets, and the quiet corners of his home.

From a young age, Hiroto showed an innate curiosity about the world, often questioning the nature of existence. It was this inquisitiveness that led him to the ancient teachings of Buddhism and Zen. However, instead of following a conventional monastic life, Hiroto chose a different path. He believed that true enlightenment wasn't secluded in monasteries, but was present in every moment of everyday life.

Hiroto's approach to Zen was practical. He practiced mindfulness while cooking, meditated while walking to the market, and found moments of deep contemplation amidst the laughter and cries of daily life. His teachings emphasized that every action, no matter how small or routine, could be a path to enlightenment if done with full awareness and intention.

As word spread about the "Zen Master of Daily Life," people from all walks of life began seeking her guidance. Hiroto's teachings resonated with many, as they were relatable and accessible. He didn't advocate for renouncing the world but rather embracing it with a clear, calm mind.

His life was a testament to the idea that enlightenment is not a distant, elusive goal but a present reality, available to all. Hiroto Takahashi's legacy continues to inspire countless individuals, reminding them that in the ordinary lies the extraordinary.

In a surprising turn of events, Hiroto's profound wisdom took on an unexpected avatar - that of a panda. The character of the panda, with its calm demeanour and thoughtful gaze, embodied Hiroto's principles perfectly. As this panda wandered through various situations, it tackled challenges with the same mindfulness and presence Hiroto preached, making Zen concepts accessible and relatable.

BONUS #1
Exclusive Offer

Send an Email and Receive a FREE eBook!

Dear Reader!

We're excited to announce a special promotion exclusively
for our valued customers like you!

If you send us an email
at hirototakahashiauthor@gmail.com,
you will receive a complimentary ebook!
It's our way of showing appreciation for your support.

Don't miss out on this limited-time offer.
Drop us an email today, and let the literary journey begin!

Warm regards,

Hiroto Takahashi.

BONUS #2
Meditation
& Mindfulness
Material

Dear Reader!

If you found joy and insight in these pages,
please take a moment to share your thoughts
with a review.:)

We're thrilled you've embarked on this journey with us.
As a token of our appreciation, we've curated exclusive
collection of meditation videos, mindfulness resources,
insightful personal reflections and much more just for you.

Scan the QR code below

Happy meditating!

Made in United States
Troutdale, OR
04/05/2024

18981914R00050